I hope the
writings in the book
will touch your heart
as they have touched mine
They reflect the thoughts of
a woman as a new bride:
through the realities of life.
Merry Christmas!
Marsha
12/25/98

Things Pondered

From the Heart of a Lesser Woman

Beth Moore

BROADMAN
&HOLMAN
PUBLISHERS

Nashville, Tennessee

Published by Broadman & Holman Publishers, Nashville, Tennessee
Design and layout ~ Tribe Design
Photography ~ Tim Bisagno

ISBN 0805401660

First Edition 1995

Dewey Decimal Classification: 242.64
Subject Heading: DEVOTIONAL LITERATURE\CHRISTIAN LIFE—
POETRY

Unless otherwise noted, Scripture quotations are from the Holy Bible,
New International Version, copyright © 1973, 1978, 1984 by
International Bible Society.

Library of Congress Cataloging-in-Publication Data

Moore, Beth, 1957–
    Things pondered: from the heart of a lesser woman/Beth Moore
        p. cm.
    ISBN 0-8054-0166-0 (hardcover)
    1. Christian life—Baptist authors. 2. Moore, Beth, 1957–
I. Title.
BV4501.2.M5767 1997
286'.1'092—dc21
    [B]   97–17520
                                                             CIP

98 99 00 01 6 5 4 3

To my mother
Whose feverish love for a word
fitly spoken endlessly inspires my own.
This offering is as much from her as to her.

"And Mary treasured up all these things and pondered them in her heart."

Luke 2:19

Introduction

They were disappointed the moment they saw her. She even cried like a girl. They wanted a boy. That didn't mean they wouldn't love her. It just meant they were like every other set of Hebrew parents, hoping they would be the ones. They had no idea they had just given birth to the mother of God.

They named her Mary. The name meant "bitter." It was a name which may have described her calling but it did not define her character. Little more than a child herself, she received the stunning news of the angel with grace and humility. Likely, Gabriel was relieved that he did not encounter the same insult he had with Zechariah. No wonder Elizabeth had exclaimed, "As soon as the sound of your greeting reached my ears, the baby in my womb leaped for joy. Blessed is she who believed...!" Her husband hadn't believed and not a single murmur from his lips had reached her ears in six months.

Mary had run to her the moment she had received the news. She hadn't hurried to her mother, father, nor friends nor fiancée. She had run to Elizabeth. How tender the God who shared with her through an angel that someone nearby could relate. The two women had one important predicament in common—questionable pregnancies, sure to stir up some talk. Elizabeth hadn't been out of the house in months. It makes you wonder why. As happy as she was, it must have been strange not to blame her sagging figure and bumpy thighs on the baby. And to think she was forced to borrow maternity clothes from her friends' granddaughters. But maybe Elizabeth and Mary were too busy talking between themselves to pay much attention. Can you imagine their conversation over tea? One too old, the other too young. One married to an old priest, the other promised to a young carpenter. One heavy with child, the other with no physical evidence to fuel her faith. But God had graciously given them one another with a bond to braid their lives forever.

Women are like that, aren't they? We long to find someone who has been where we've been, who shares our fragile places, who sees our sunsets with the same shades of blue. Soulmates. They somehow validate the depth of our experiences. It is doubtful we have experienced much to which Mary could not relate. Through the course of her journey on this planet, she would experience fear, rejection, loneliness, disappointment, and heart break. She would know what it was like to have one child so entirely different from her others. She would battle sibling rivalry and yearn for her children to love one another. She would one day urge her oldest son to reach his potential, and although He would question her timing, He would nonetheless perform the miracle she requested. She would also confront her evolving role as the mother of an adult son. He would be no longer at her constant beck and call. And, ultimately, the woman highly favored by God would have to consider if the risk of loving was worth the risk of losing. Her small, suffering frame at the scene of her Son's death would prove to be testimony. One day, all those things would come. But in the meantime, as a young girl, she made something her practice that far surpassed her age or experience. She learned to catch a moment in her hand before it flew away and hold it tightly while she had the chance.

Luke's gospel (chap. 2) tells it like this...

"And there were in the same country shepherds abiding in the field, keeping watch over their flock by night. And, lo, the angel of the Lord came upon them, and the glory of the Lord shone round about them—and they were sore afraid. And the angel said unto them, Fear not— for, behold, I bring you good tidings of great joy, which shall be to all people. For unto you is born this day in the city of David a Savior, which is Christ the Lord. And this shall be a sign unto you; Ye shall find the babe wrapped in swaddling clothes, lying in a manger. And suddenly there was with the angel a multitude of the heavenly host praising God, and saying, Glory to God in the highest, and on earth peace, good will toward men. And it came to pass, as the angels were gone away from them into heaven, the shepherds said one to another, Let us now go even unto Bethlehem, and see this thing which is come to pass, which the Lord hath made known unto us. And they came with haste, and found Mary, and Joseph, and the babe lying in a manger. And when they had seen it, they made known abroad the saying which was told them concerning this child. And all they that heard it wondered at those things which were told them by the shepherds."

And what about the young virgin mother?

> "But Mary treasured up all these things
> and pondered them in her heart."

Pondered. It's a wonderful word. It is the practice of casting many things together, combining them and considering them as one. In that moment, a host of memories must have been dancing in her head. The angel's appearance. His words. Her flight to the hill country of Judea. Elizabeth's greeting. Their late night conversations. The first time she noticed her tummy was rounding. Joseph's face when he saw her. The way she felt when he believed. The whispers of neighbors. The doubts of her parents. The first time she felt the baby move inside of her. The dread of the long trip. The reality of being full term, bouncing on the back of a beast. The first pain. The fear of having no place to bear a child. The horror of the nursery. The way it looked. The way it smelled. The way He looked. God so frail. So tiny. So perfect. Love so abounding. Grace so amazing. Wise men bowed down. Shepherds made haste. Each memory like treasures in a box. She gathered the jewels, held them to her breast, and engraved them on her heart forever.

The following pages are my responses to her worthy example. Words from a life absent of her lofty calling and excellent character. Experiences of an average woman, wife, and mother written to invite you to remember your own.

These are things pondered.

Family
Traces

12

Wedding Bells

I should have been ready. It was an event I had prepared for all my life. But right at that moment, my wedding dress itched, my hair was bushier than my veil, and I couldn't get to a mirror for my bridesmaids. It was just as well. I was bound to be disappointed that the glamour of a film star was not included in the rental of my wedding gown.

This was not the way my sister, Gay, and I had played it. We had hosted at least a thousand rehearsal dinners with our Barbies and a bag of fritos. Calendaring was certainly not the problem. I had always known that I would marry at Christmas of my twenty first year. (That's how old Mother told me Barbie was. According to Mother, she had finished college before she married Ken.) I never had a wedding dress for my Barbie but Mom had given me the most beautiful red velvet dress for her I had ever seen. I used it instead which is exactly why she always had to have a Christmas wedding. Sure enough, it was December 30th and although I had on a traditional candlelight gown, my six bridesmaids were enchanting in their red Christmas dresses with capes, all carrying lanterns.

The groom also wasn't the problem. I knew he had to be from God. He came along the closest to the magical marrying age and my college graduation and God forbid I would graduate without a proper betrothal. And more importantly, he was the spitting image of Ken. This qualification was not a conscious test at the time; however, it never occurred to me I'd marry anyone who was not tall, dark, and handsome. He certainly fit that bill and he was the perfect companion for my Texas hair. Yes, the timing and the twosome seemed to be a match. Still, I had this sneaking suspicion welling up inside of me that I might be in for a slight shock.

The lightning bolt of a lifetime struck about one week later when we returned from our honeymoon to the old place we were renting from my father-in-law for free. Conspicuously absent was the portrait of me in my wedding gown over a blazing fireplace. In fact, the closest thing we had to a fireplace was the furnace to the left of the commode. The one I kept falling into because the seat was always up. There was no dishwasher, no garbage disposal, and no money. The only thing that house had plenty of was deer heads. They were everywhere. And they seemed to stare at me as if I had sold out. They did lead to the purchase of a secondhand dryer, however. Keith bought one the day after he came in with a friend and found our underwear dangling from their horns. I think that may have been the first time anyone had ever called me "sacrilegious."

My groom was not very impressed with playing grown-ups either. He took a cut in pay when he went from Daddy's allowance to hourly wages. He worked long hours out in the heat and worked with people who had no teeth. Then he'd walk in the door, say he was starving and look at me as if he expected me to do something about it. Think as I may, I cannot for the life of me remember a kitchen in the Barbie Dream House. Then it hit me. I wasn't Barbie. He wasn't Ken. This was no dream. And I wanted my mother. Now that I'm a parent, I have a feeling she wanted me, too, but she didn't let on. If I'd had a car that I didn't have to push to start, I might have been out of there. But there I was and there he was and even "making the best of it" seemed a dismal prospect. Had God not given us both the uncanny ability to laugh at inappropriate times, I don't think we could have made it. There were many months when we either laughed or cried, smooched or didn't speak. There was little in between.

We've suffered our share of bumps and bruises over the years since we drove off in our Barbie dream car and had a head on collision with reality. We've grown up a little and grown together a lot. We had entered marriage each carrying a deluxe, five piece set of emotional baggage, certain our own was heavier than the other's. We had expectations which exceeded the realm of possibility. I have finally forgiven Keith for not being Ken. I've almost forgiven myself for not being Barbie. And by the grace of God, we've made it in spite of ourselves.

Marriage is a serious matter. It is often embraced with less prayer than a college exam. I feel rather certain that the chief reason a Believer often enters marriage void of fervent prayer is because inherent in the asking is His right to answer us. And once we've made up our minds, a "no" or a "wait" from God is out of the question. Like us, you may have "accidentally" fallen into the marriage God had intended for you. Like us, you may have also suffered the penalty for not having built your relationship upon Him from the very beginning. And perhaps, like us, you're learning.

To marry without the blatant inclusion of Christ is to have entirely missed the point. In Ephesians 5:31 the Apostle Paul quotes the original wedding vows God spoke over the very first marriage all the way back in the Garden...

> "For this reason a man will leave his father and mother and be united to his wife, and the two will become one flesh."

In Ephesians 5:32, thousands of years after God instituted marriage, He revealed its lofty purpose...

"This is a profound mystery—but I am talking about Christ and the church."

Marriage is sacred. It was created to be the wedding portrait of Christ and His Bride hung over the blazing fireplace of judgment. A match made in Heaven, a contract signed in blood. In the bond of marriage, we are to stand at the altar of Sacrifice or we're not to stand at all.

Colossians 1:16,17 gives us this assurance—

"...by him all things were created...and in him all things hold together."

God alone created marriage. Adam slept through the entire ceremony. Eve came in late. It seems to me men are still sleeping through marriage and women are still coming to their senses a little too late. God alone performed that ceremony and He alone can hold it together.

Much of our disillusionment over marriage stems from the fact that we've been duped into believing that good equals easy. In other words, we often assume that if something is difficult, it can't be of God. Nothing has been more difficult for Christ than the marriage to His Bride yet Jude 24 says He'll present her to His Father with great joy! The Greek root word is "Agalliao." It means "to show one's joy by leaping and skipping denoting excessive or ecstatic joy and delight!"* Just picture it. After all the ups and downs in the relationship, after all the marriage has cost Him, He'll act like a love-struck boy introducing his girl to his dad for the very first time. Why? Because He thinks she was worth it.

On the pleasant days of marriage, gaze across at your groom and conclude he is worth it. On the difficult days of marriage gaze *up* at your Groom and conclude *He's* worth it.

"A cord of three strands is not quickly broken."

Ecclesiastes 4:12b

*The Complete Word Study Dictionary of the New Testament, compiled and edited by Spiros Zodhiates, Th.D., World Bible Publishers, Inc., Iowa Falls, Iowa. Copyright June 1992. p.64.

16

Dear Bride To Be

Come to me, Dear Bride to be,
And kneel before My Throne
And I will share My heart with you
And make your house a home.
Listen well, lean closely
There are secrets at My feet—
The marriage you will soon begin
This Bridegroom will complete.

The man with whom you'll journey
Is your wedding gift from me
To teach you things beyond this world...
A precious mystery.
Bearing all these things in mind
You'll never lack for wealth
For through your union I will choose
To teach you of Myself.

Let him hold you tightly
And keep you safe from harm
Until I'll one day hold you
In My everlasting arms.
Let him wipe your tears away
And trust him with your pain
Until I wipe them all away
And Heaven is your gain.

Pray to love his tender touch
And want his gentle kiss
I grant you both my blessing
And ask you not to miss
The reason why I've chosen
For two halves to become one—
That you might see the Bride of Christ,
Sweet Daughter and Dear Son.

So make his home a refuge
He's to love you as I do
Until your mansion is complete...
A place prepared for you.
And if I should choose to leave you here
When I have called him home
Trust I'll be your husband near...
You'll never be alone.

Babies

Early one morning only eight weeks after the day we married, I heard an oddly controlled voice ascend from the kitchen. "It's positive, Beth. It came out positive."

"That's impossible," I thought. After all, my doctor had assured me that birth control would be a waste of time. I was told that the fashion in which God had fearfully and wonderfully made me would make conception an impossibility without medical intervention. I was certain that the demands of marriage, i.e., cooking and cleaning, had made me understandably ill. I went to the kitchen to see for myself. There it was. The first sign of our first offspring—a jagged circle in the bottom of a glass test tube. I screamed. Then I laughed. Then I jumped up and down all over the linoleum. I had wanted a baby since the time I had been one. It was not until I threw my arms around my husband that I realized he was either terrified or had died standing up.

I set an extra place at the table that night and left it there until it was occupied. I immediately poked my stomach out as far as I could and practiced waddling in front of the mirror. And, most importantly, I enrolled in a child development course at the nearby community college. I planned to be the most wonderful mother in the world. Second only to the Blessed Mother herself. I never missed a single class and spoke as an authority on every point. I rolled my eyes at the ignorance of many of my classmates. It was clear they had not acquired the depth of experience I had while babysitting. Among the host of vows I made before my class, two were priority— I would *never* spank and I would *never* say, "Because I said so." I was the fourth of five Army brats and the first one in line to ask "WHY?" The tip of my father's index finger and those four words were stamped indelibly in my gray matter. I would be a far different kind of parent. I would simply explain things to my children. I would draw them up to my level and speak to them like little adults. I would patiently escort them to understanding and bask in the success of my modern methods. The course ended. I felt it was a shame the teacher could not give an "A+" on a report card. An "A" seemed so common.

I quickly enrolled in another class. It was called "Lamaze Guide to Natural Childbirth." My husband had warmed up to the idea of starting a family due to the rapidly growing evidence that it was inevitable. He dutifully attended each one of our classes and fell asleep every night to my breathing exercises and stuck as closely to my side as my anti-stretch mark cream. I had highlighted my lime green Lamaze manual in fluorescent

colors and worn the ink off the pages instructing how to
experience minimal pain. I was not into pain. I was also
far too contemporary to consider any drugs. I was
expecting my first child at the exact moment the partum
pendulum had swung from being knocked out to all
natural. I was convinced that if I took one iota of pain
reliever, my child would not only grow up to take drugs,
she would likely sell Heroin on the nearest corner. I
hadn't made an "A" in Child Development for nothing. I
made my husband promise that no matter how I begged,
he would not let me take any medication. I faithfully
practiced my "hee hee" breathing and braced myself for
the big day. And a big day it was sure to be. I had
already caught a glimpse of myself in the stainless steel
bathtub faucet while taking a bath. My navel looked like a
helicopter pad. My stomach looked like the Astrodome
and my head and arms looked like they were down a few
more exits. I took showers from then on.

One Sunday morning nine months and two
weeks from our wedding, I awakened to my stomach
doing abdominals independently. I whispered my
suspicions into my husband's left ear to which he
responded by jumping straight out of the bed into his
cowboy boots. I convinced him we had plenty of time to
run by the church and let me teach a quick Sunday
School lesson to my sixth graders on the way to the
hospital. He conceded reluctantly and we made a bee line
for the church. I've never been known to teach a short
lesson and by the time we headed back home to grab my
suitcase, the contractions were growing powerfully.
Nothing in Houston, Texas is vaguely close by and our
hospital was considered far even according to our
standards. As we began our trek, I said to Keith, "It sure
is a good thing I practiced my Lamaze as much as I did.
This really hurts. Don't worry, though. I'm prepared and
I feel in control." Minutes passed and I was feeling a tad
less controlled.

"Keith," I suggested, "you might try taking
streets with no traffic lights. I don't think we ought to
tarry at another one." By this time I was "hee hee"
breathing.

A few minutes later, as my sweet husband began
to panic, I said, "You stop again and you deliver this
kid!" By this time my feet were on the dash board. With
eyes that could shoot torpedoes, I selected Keith's face as
my focal point and announced emphatically, "I'M
READY TO PUSH!" We pulled up in front of
Rosewood Hospital on two wheels.

My husband flew in the door and said, "Forget
the labor room. It's too late! Get her to Delivery!" A
worn out nurse with a dead pan face fetched the doctor
with the speed of molasses. I squeezed my knees
together and gritted my teeth trying to hold it off until
they got there.

The doctor arrived, examined me, and said, "Mrs. Moore, you are one and a half centimeters dilated." It was a long day.

I divorced Keith during every contraction and remarried him in between. I didn't know a soul could feel pain like that and live and I was taking him with me if I didn't. My "hee hee" breathing had diminished to sobs of "He He made me do this!" Many hours and a large incision later, I gave birth. I don't know why they call it "expecting." There is nothing about it you could've expected. Her head was misshapen from the difficult delivery. Her head was bleeding from the forceps. Her cheeks were bruised from the pressure. And she was the most beautiful creature I had ever seen in all my life. Not many things in life are perfect but every now and then, every once in a great while, there arrives a perfect moment. This was one of them.

That moment gave birth to the most joyful days I had ever experienced in my life. Keith and I thought all well parented babies sat happily in their carseats, slept through the night, and bore signs of brilliancy from birth. Her name was Amanda. She talked nice and early and walked nice and late. As the infant turned into a delightfully creative toddler, her mind became a constant bed of fairy tales and her nursery turned into a palace. An obvious "Save the Whaler" from her first words, she was born to crusade righteous causes, however off the wall, and stick up for the underdog. Deep spirited from the start, she once looked into the sky at three years old and with eyes spilling tears, said, "One lonely little cloud. I wish it had some friends." By senior high school she had changed wonderfully little.

I had never spanked her nor had I ever said those four deplorable words. After all, I had made a vow. And I almost got away with it. That is, until I had that one fleeting thought when I glanced at her pink cheeks and pig tales as she swung at the neighborhood park, "I'm so good at this, it would be a shame for me not to do it again. After all, Keith wants another so badly." Just as the thought went through my head, the loudest clap of thunder I had ever heard nearly collapsed the sky. I know now that it was God having a good knee slapper.

I feel sure this was the moment when He summoned Gabriel and said, "Remember that little spirited spirit we've had around here all these centuries just waiting for the right mother? She just reported for duty."

I had no idea what God had planned. As usual, I had plans of my own. After all, planliness is next to Godliness, is it not? Without informing my husband, I plotted my next pregnancy. I planned to be in the family way by Thanksgiving just in time to give him the ultimate gift on Christmas Day. I couldn't imagine ever loving another little girl as much as I had my first and I had always heard every Father needed a son, so I chose just the right formula of words and petitioned God for a boy, in Jesus' Name...and in advance. I thought it would be simpler that way. My timing worked perfectly according to plan and by Thanksgiving I was kissing Keith as he headed out the door by 7:00 A.M. and throwing up by 8:00 A.M. I wrapped a darling, but very manly pair of blue booties in crisp red and green wrap and stuck the special delivery all the way under the Christmas tree.

December 25th finally rolled around and we gathered with extended family at my parent's home and began to exchange gifts. As forever his custom, my Father passed out every gift one by one. Finally, a single small package was under the tree. Having no idea what the present contained, he announced to my husband that it was addressed to him...from Santa Claus. Keith didn't waste much time tearing away the Christmas ribbons and paper, then stared totally puzzled at the fuzzy little booties. He finally looked at me across the room and mouthed the words, "Does this mean you want to?" I responded loudly, "No, my Darling, this means WE ARE!" He swept me up and swung me around while my family cried and I threw up. After the hysteria had died down, he inquired, "Just one more thing I'm curious about. Why are these blue booties?"

I quipped, "Because, Honey, I asked God for a boy, in Jesus' Name." How could he be so spiritually immature?

My tummy was swollen by the time I ate the second piece of pumpkin pie. I didn't care. I was filled with a complete satisfaction over well executed plans. What could be better? A handsome husband, a precious daughter, a wonderful son, and a wiener dog named Coney Island! Boy, was I feeling sassy.

Seven months into the pregnancy the obstetrics nurse, who was a friend of mine, offered to do a sonogram for which she had been recently trained. I drank the four and a half gallons of water required and sloshed all the way to the doctor's office. She smeared the monitor with a clear, ice cold jelly then whacked it on my tummy pushing as hard as she could on my bladder. She positioned the television screen right in front of me and we began to watch a performance of award winning caliber. It was a miracle. The child flipped and turned and sucked its thumb. We saw everything! The eyes, the nose, the fingers and toes! Everything but one. After thirty minutes of Star Search, I finally said, "Have you been able to tell he's a boy yet?"

She responded reluctantly, "No, I just can't seem to get the right angle."

That baby didn't have an angle we hadn't seen. I retorted, "You're telling me a story. That baby's a girl!"

"You're absolutely right."

I went home, sat on the couch and looked up at God. "You can change this, You know. You can either do it now or You can do it right in front of the labor and delivery staff. I don't care when or how, just do it!" I added one little footnote. "But if You're going to do it, be sure You do it all the way." I didn't need anything else to worry about. I positioned myself very still to see if I'd feel anything. I didn't.

It wasn't that I didn't want another daughter. I love little girls! It's that I had shot off my big mouth to everyone this side of the Pecos and I was far too pregnant to be sitting out on any limb. Somehow I had a feeling God had made up His mind. I broke the news apologetically to my husband. After a moment, he chuckled and asked, "Am I supposed to be disappointed or something?" That was all I needed to hear. The next two months we ecstatically prepared for daughter number two. When I say we prepared, surely you're believing by now, *we prepared!* This time I passed on the Lamaze classes and entered the hospital with my "Say Yes to Drugs" T-shirt chanting those three magic words, "Just say yes!" The way I saw it, bugs and turnips were "natural" and I didn't like them either.

I never could tell that the anesthesia I had longed for had any effect at all until a few moments after I struggled and gave birth to that wonderful child. I awakened in the recovery room to my husband's tender words as he whispered in the tiny ear of his Christmas gift. She was dark complected like my "Ken" and had a white gauze cap on her head.He had her propped in his left hand and was holding up one little slat of the mini-blinds with the other. Her little eyes squinted as he promised, "It's a mighty big world out there, but don't you worry. It won't hurt you. Daddy will be right there." It was a perfect moment. My second.

That beautiful child was an angel from Heaven for two solid weeks when she abruptly opened her mouth and, to date, has not shut it. I began to have a vague recollection of that mighty clap of thunder on the pinnacle day of my piety. She sat way too early. She crawled way too early and she ran way too early. She has yet to learn to walk. When her screams turned into vocabulary, she was finally able to put her frustrations into words. The first sentence out of her mouth is accurately recorded in her baby book—"Don't boss me!" Melissa has never been one to take sides. She came to take over.

We could always tell what kind of day it was going to be by the way her hair looked when she walked down the stairs in the morning. If she had experienced a rough night, it was going to be a rough day. We tried cutting her hair nice and short but she still came down those stairs looking just like an angry banny rooster. Then came that fated day when she was four years old and demanded to go outside on a cold, rainy day. I said no. She asked why. I explained why. She said no. I explained again. She threw a fit again. "But WHY can't I, Mom?? You're just plain ole mean!" Just then, I felt a strange allergic reaction occurring around my mouth. It felt as like ants were crawling all over my tongue. My lips began to blow. Then it happened. I couldn't control it. It just happened. In a compulsory refrain, I screamed, "BECAUSE I SAID SO!" Once was not enough. Every single one stored up inside me came out in a flash. I yelled it at the dog. I yelled it at the cat. I yelled it at the swing set. I yelled it sharp and flat. It was freedom! Liberation to my soul! Free at last! I fell exhausted on the couch at which point my older child said with hands on her hips to her precocious little sister, "Because she said so. That's why." To which she responded, "Oh. Okay." And she skipped away. When answers aren't enough, there is "Because I said so." Thanks, Major Dad.

Her stubbornness is half her charm. One day after Mother's Day Out, she announced to me proudly, "My teacher called me a different drummer!" I was furious. I knew what that teacher had really said. "Melissa sure marches to the beat of a different drummer." Just about the time I started to turn right back around and give that teacher a piece of my mind, I thought about the words Melissa had quoted. Her teacher said it one way. She heard it quite another. She didn't march to anyone's beat. She *was* the different drummer. And she still is.

I marvel at the ignorance of a mother who thought two daughters might be too much alike to enjoy. Their appearances were strikingly similar but their personalities were gloriously unique from the start. One lived in a fairy tale. The other a tail spin. One cradled a red and black lady bug in her palm and said, "Oh, my pretty little ladybug." The other, half her size, looked over her shoulder and retorted, "It's dead, stupid." One aimed to please. The other aimed to push. One was my favorite. And so was the other.

Only God could have created a parent's love. Only to God can we all be His favorite, the "apple of His eye." (Ps. 17:8) How can we ever doubt that He loves us as much as another if we, as human parents, are capable of the same? What unfathomable depths of love must be in the heart of One who said,

> "If you, then, though you are evil, know how to give good gifts to your children, how much more will your Father in heaven give good gifts to those who ask him!"

Matthew 7:11

I would give my children anything I could afford if only it wouldn't hurt them. He gave us everything He could afford—the riches of Heaven—His Son, and oh, how it hurt Him.

Today, with daughters I have to literally look up to, I arrive at the same conclusion I suspected many years ago when I danced with glee over my first babysitting job. I like children.

I Like Children

I like the way they're always full of
surprises…how they have a mind of their own from the
very beginning and arrive just in time to be two weeks
late. I like the way they look like little strangers the
moment you feast your eyes on them…totally
unrecognizable yet freshly detached from your own body.
I like the way they come to your hospital room in a plain
white blanket, wrapped so tightly and with such precision
you wonder if they'll have to wear it to college. I like
how they look in their baby bed the very first time you
tuck them in it—so small you decide they better sleep in
your room. I like the funny expressions they make while
they're dozing and how they crack an awkward smile as if
they've tagged an angel. I like the way they yawn with
their whole bodies and how the stork bites on the backs
of their necks are often as plain as day. I like the way they
never go for the apple sauce disguising the pureed liver. I
like how they smell after their grannies bathe them and
bring them to their mamas. I like the soft bristles of their
brushes and how their hair looks when you first get it to
part. I like the way they love you more than anyone else
on earth has ever loved you. I like how they quiet to *your*
whisper after all your friends and relatives have
desperately tried to calm them. I like the first time they
reach their arms out to you. I like having the prerogative
not to lay them down for a nap and rocking them instead
for all three hours if you have a mind to.

I like the way they learn to entertain all the
patrons at the restaurant with a spoon on the metal tray
of a high chair. I like how they first say Mama and Dada
with twenty syllables each. I like the dimples their knees
make when they first learn to stand. I like how they learn
to walk because they want to get to *you*. And, boy, do I
like footie pajamas…until the next morning when no
telling what is in the footie. I like the way they know
they're going to Mother's Day Out the instant they wake
up. And they're not in the mood. And I *love* sleepy hair.
You know…how it looks all fuzzy on one side when they
first wake up.

I like the sudden discovery of sentences as their
thoughts take the form of endless, delightful vocabulary. I
like how you nearly die laughing once you realize what
they're trying to say. I like the way neighbors don't
realize they've just been insulted because they can't
understand a word out of their mouths. I like the way
"R's" don't appear in their alphabet until they are at least
five years old. I like their simple rules of
socialization…move or I push…gimme or I bite.

I like how little girls think pink chiffon dresses
are divine and little boys wear their cowboy boots with

shorts. I like the way little girls prefer umbrellas and little boys—puddles. I like how they look on the first day of kindergarten—from the front. Not from the back. I like taking pictures of them with their friends every year on the first day of school...that is, until you come across that very first one in the drawer. And you cry. 'Cause it went too fast. And you can't go back. I like the way they know it's time to go even when Mommy doesn't agree. Because that's the way it should be.

I like how your children like you even better when they're grown. And how, if you're really lucky, they might have children of their own. And you can try it once more.

And maybe do a little better. Because I like children.

When my daughters were seven and ten and we were basking in the marvelous years between preschool and adolescence, I learned a life changing lesson about prayer—God reserves the right to fill petitions you forgot to cancel long after you thought you changed your mind. All those years ago when I had asked God for a son, I assumed His answer was "no," not "wait." Boy, was I ever wrong. On February 14, 1990, my husband gave me a Valentine's gift that keeps on giving—a pint sized four year old orphaned boy. He was the most beautiful little guy I had ever seen in all my life. I've since arrived at the conclusion that God often makes children who are going to be extra work extra cute. At the time, however, his big brown eyes and inch long eye lashes were simply selling points. God had reserved room in our hearts and a room in our home for one more child. We were not looking to adopt a little boy. We were very satisfied with the size of our family. God had tendered our hearts over the plight of only one. His birth parents were married when he was born, but they soon gave up on each other and ultimately him. Sadly, the marriage of his second guardians also collapsed and they sought a family to raise him. His name was Michael but the girls soon nick named him "Spud" and it stuck. He was darling, very troubled, and the spitting image of his new Daddy.

These next words are not just phrases and rhymes. They comprise the events of a night that dramatically changed our lives. It was late that evening and our daughters were in bed. And, yes, it was a perfect moment. Our third. Our son.

The Adoption

I heard the front door open
My heart began to pound
I froze to see if it was them
Then I heard the sound

Of a tiny little four year old
Asking this strange man
"How come we gathered all my clothes?"
Did my husband have a plan

Exactly how to tell the child
On this awaited day
"You've left the only house you've known
And now you're here to stay?"

And what am *I* to say to him,
"Hello, my name is Mom?"
I was filled with insecurity
But my husband looked so calm

He diverted his attention
And didn't answer right away
He looked at me assuredly
"Let's just let him play."

After minutes crept and crawled away
He patted his right knee.
"Can I talk to you a moment, Child?
Would you sit right here with me?"

He stopped what he was doing
And crawled up on his lap
He looked straight into my husband's face
And dropped his baseball cap.

"Michael, do you have a Dad?"
My heart jumped in my throat.
A sadness swept that precious face
"No," he said, "I don't."

"Michael, I've been thinking
Since the first I saw of you
We've got a common problem
Is there something we can do?"

"I've everything that I could want
Upon my list but one.
It seems that you don't have a Dad
And I don't have a son."

"Whatcha say we strike a deal
And seal it with a shake?
I've thought it over carefully
Now, the choice is *yours* to make."

I remember well the boy's words,
Feet swinging as he sat—
After all this time without a Dad,
"It happens just like that?"

The man gave him a gentle nod
The boy's grin grew wet
As if he thought, "What's there to lose?"
He blurted out, "You bet!"

His hand appeared so fragile
In my husband's callused palm
Keith whispered, "There's a bonus here.
That lady's now your Mom!"

The handshake gave way to a hug
Tears came as no surprise
Transfixed, I watched my precious son
Be born before my eyes.

They ascended up our stairway
Suitcase tightly in his hand
My husband pointed to a door
And said, "Enter, little man."

Cautiously he took each step
Until he was inside
Bunk beds for boys, and lots of toys
Confused, his eyes grew wide

"Whose stuff is this?" The boy inquired
Not knowing what to do
"Go ahead and touch it, Child!
It all belongs to you."

The birthday of our special son
Should not seem strange or new
For if you have been born again
You've been adopted, too.

For God so loves this aching world
He pulls us, good and bad,
On to His lap and says to us,
"I want to be your Dad."

"You have no Heavenly Father
And you're not my son, it's true,
But there's room inside my family
A space made just for you."

"It's not a snap decision
It's the kind that takes the heart
But with a 'yes' all things are new
Want a second start?"

"You bet, Dear Lord, my mind's made up.
I've made my final choice
Yes, I'll be your brand new son!"
Let angels now rejoice!

"Partake, Joint Heir, your heritage...
I am your great Reward
Stick closely by my side, Dear Child
I'll guard you with my sword!"

Friend, are you wandering lost about,
An orphan of the soul,
Bleeding from your brokenness?
But One can make you whole.

Cease waiting 'til you're good enough
There's nothing you can do
God's business is adoption, Child,
And He has chosen you.

Forsake the earthly vanities
No treasure's left to own
That equals that sweet moment when
God says, "Child, welcome home."

31

Panic

Within just a few days I saw signs obvious to any Mother that Michael had been traumatized. He did not express the normal emotions of a four-year-old. No matter how badly he was hurt, he did not cry. It was little wonder. Even the few facts we knew would have been enough to scar a child for a lifetime without the mercy and intervention of God. Tears had not helped him much through neglect, continuous abandonment, constant conflict, broken promises, harsh punishment and an early introduction to the police and Child Protective Services. He was in emotional shambles.

Not only did he seem void of tears, he was void of laughter. No matter how silly his new sisters acted, he rarely smiled. He had no appetite except for things and there were never enough of them to satisfy his emptiness. He entered our home on the basis of one assumption— sooner or later we would leave him, too, and he'd just as soon cut to the chase. It seemed to become his goal in life to hasten the inevitable.

He required the focus of all attention and within a very short time was terribly threatened by the two children who had preceded him there. If either of our daughters came to me for attention, he would find a very effective way to seize it for himself. At the same time he craved my focus, he also remained strangely detached. He seemed to have very little feeling for me until night time when he would hold my head in a death grip and drop off to sleep chanting, "Please, Mommy, don't leave me."

Michael suffered constant bouts of deep depression that would ultimately turn to fits of violence and anger. Emotion finally emerged with frightening velocity. Our neighbors would not let their children play with him. His preschool teachers could not deal with him. We tucked our tails and ran as fast as we could to a Godly child psychologist who met with him four times. The fifth appointment she found me in the waiting room instead of Michael. In near hysteria, I cried, "Help me. Teach me. He needs a counselor twenty-four hours a day and I'm the only one there."

By this time our other children were traumatized, too. Like their mother, they had envisioned the adoption to be a glorious romance and found themselves, instead, being displaced by a child who was ready to seize attention at all costs. They had tried their hardest to reach out to him. One day Amanda was trying to get Michael to draw. We had often tried to get him to express himself on paper only to see him scribble angrily until the paper was torn to shreds. We were too ignorant to realize he *was* expressing himself.

This particular day she changed the proposal to one that would meet with his approval. "Michael, look at the stick man Sissy drew." He glanced at her drawing and cracked a tiny smile. She continued, "If I draw *you* a stick man, will you just fill in the face? That's all. Just draw eyes and a nose and a mouth. I know you can do it. Show me how." To our amazement, he nodded his head and we all stood around him with great anticipation. This would be the first picture Michael had ever drawn in his life. The face he drew on that stick man, he also drew on my mind forever. The mouth was turned down and lines of tears streamed from the eyes. We all sat and stared. Amanda had the maturity to say, however sadly, "That's really good, Spud. Really good. Thank you." I excused myself from the table, went into my room, put my head under my pillow and sobbed. At that very moment I knew that precious child needed more than we had. Why hadn't God given him to parents who really knew what they were doing? Who didn't have other children? Who didn't have such demanding lives already?? This one was beyond me. It was the most terrifying season of my adult life.

Could It Be?

Empty eyes, a fragile heart
Where to begin? How do I start?
Consider the risk! The pain's too intense!
I can't be the one. This doesn't make sense.

Even his sleep isn't peaceful or sound
From a crack in the door light casts on a frown.
He's made up his mind by the time he is four
Too much behind him...too little in store.

A smile so rare, his words so few
I study expressions, they offer no clue
No laugh when he's tickled, no cry when he's hurt
Won't run ahead nor hide in my skirt.

Desperate for playmates but unable to play
A few moments pass, they all run away
Surrounded by people, he's still all alone
No sense of family, no sense of home.

In one breath he utters, "Please, Mommy, don't leave."
Then he shoves me away, my heart starts to bleed
The walls go up, he slams the door
Never wanted me less, never needed me more.

Can't you see, I'm torn to shreds?
Precious lives at stake in nearby beds
Courage melting, what have we done?
Satan fights dirty...sometimes he's won.

So many questions shout in my mind
You make no mistakes but maybe this time
You entrusted too much and caught us off guard
Or could it be
Your perfect will
Is sometimes just this hard?

Fresh out of methods, struck out on my plans
Nowhere to quit...can't wash my hands
Filled with self-hatred, hanging my head
God lifted my chin then gently said,
But,
Can you just love him?

Questions

I'll never forget the moment I knew God was asking me that simple question, "Can you just love him?" It was the night I had come to the end of my strength. Keith and I had tried to get away for a weekend to catch our breath. My parents had offered to babysit our boy and it had been disastrous. Keith's parents were equally concerned for us and our friends wondered what we had done. We felt as if we were sitting all alone in a sinking boat. After he had gone to sleep that night, the rest of us sat on our oldest daughter's bed, held each other and cried. Our daughters were growing resentful and felt like they couldn't get to us any more. We were stretched to the point of ripping.

Later that night when we were all alone, I laid down the law to Keith. "If we happen to be strong enough to pull him up, he stays. But if he is strong enough to pull us down, he goes. I will not have my other children traumatized because of a child who refuses to be helped." Keith stood up and walked out the front door. He looked up and down the street then walked back into the house. "What are you doing?" I asked angrily.

"I'm looking for the next set of parents in line and I don't see a single volunteer. Elizabeth, this child has been abandoned over and over again. We told him we wouldn't be like them. This is his last stop."

I burst into tears, "Then what are we going to do?"

Before Keith could say a word, I heard it. The voice of God speaking loudly…speaking directly into the depths of my heart. "Can you just love him?"

He could have asked me a multitude of questions I could have readily answered—

"Can you make sure he's educated at the best schools?"

"Yes, Sir, I can."

"Can you always dress him to look his best?"

"You bet I can, Sir! He'll be the best dressed in his class!"

"Can you take him to church?"

"Without a doubt, I can!"

"How about Disney World?"

"Consider it done, Sir!"

But that's not what He asked.

"Can you just love him? Really love him? With a love that never fails?"

Before I knew what had happened, Keith was pulling me up the stairs saying, "We're going to pray over him, that's what!" I practically crawled up those stairs, totally exhausted physically and emotionally. We asked God to leave Michael in a deep sleep as He had Abram when He made a covenant over him. The covenant we needed to make was between God and the two of us. We placed our hands on that sleeping boy and mustered up the little strength we had left and cried out for help. We admitted to our utter helplessness, our worthless naiveté, and our extreme disappointment. We claimed that boy for Christ that day like we never had before and we invited the enemy who had slipped in our house through a crack in the foundation out of our home. We walked down those stairs feeling centuries old.

It wasn't the next day. It was so gradual, I couldn't even tell you exactly when it was. But one day things began to change. In bits and pieces. In glimpses and glances. Somewhere along the way, we became his parents.

From Where I Am

Three years have come, three years have gone
Sometimes it seems short, sometimes it seems long
Never had so much doubt, never made such mistakes
Nor had so much worry nor kept so awake

Three steps forward and two steps back
A life full of grays...I like white and black
Don't know how he seems from up where You are
But this is the guy I see in my yard—

A hand full of frogs, a hose in the other
He struts to the meter to flush out another
Eyes once so empty, now full of mischief
Jean pockets bulging with all kinds of kid's stuff

One shoe on the porch the other is missing
Ears prop his cap, they're sure not for listening
He'll fish at the pond if time will afford
With a baseball nearby in case he gets bored.

His room is cluttered with artwork from school
He likes high tops and haircuts that make him look cool
He'd gladly dump school, thanks all the same,
'Til he walks down the hall, and kids call him by name.

Just when I've lost it, frazzled and frantic
He swipes flowers from the neighbor's,
                            he's such a romantic
Paddled a plenty, his feet stomp the floor
I'll think that it's settled, he'll try me once more.

We've read lots of books and fought lots of fears
We've talked our mouths dry and shed lots of tears
"Mommy, did you miss me before I moved in?"
And, "I want to be born from *your* tummy like them!"

We've come a long way with a long way to go
No clues for the future, so much I don't know
Will he ever trust You to set his soul free?
Or realize the teacher that he's been to me?

I'm not all alone where answers are due
I recall, there's an answer I still owe to You
Three years have vanished, It's time to confess You asked,
            "Can you just love him?"

Yes, Lord, Oh yes.

Love

The Greeks called it "Agape." God called it a supernatural expression and something only He can do. But He does it through hearts vacated by their own responses and made available for His. Agape is a kind of love God demonstrates *to* one person *through* another. Romans 5:8 gives us the perfect example, "But God demonstrates his own love (Agape) for us in that while we were yet sinners, Christ died for us."

In other words, God loved us through Christ. His Word also says, "As I have loved you, so you must love one another" (John 13:34). Just as He demonstrated His love to us through Christ, God desires to demonstrate His love to others through *us*.

No doubt, God has placed you in the position to love the unlovely, whether or not you've been obedient to that command. In fact, I think that we can surmise that any one among us who is not struggling with loving someone isn't getting out enough! It's one of His priority agendas. He wants to use us to love with a supernatural supply someone we never could love otherwise. No Believer can avoid this crucial high calling. Agape is an obedient response of availability to God, not a feeling. But, although it is not a feeling, its ultimate end is a feeling. You'll never respond to God with the mind of Christ that you do not finally end up with the heart of Christ. It's nothing less than supernatural. A pure, unadulterated miracle. See it for yourself—"Love never fails" (1 Cor. 13:8).

You may ask, "Does it never fail the giver or the receiver?" It fails neither. For the receiver, they will never have been loved for nothing. God is very practical. If He has called upon you to be His vessel of love toward someone else, it is because He has a plan. If you are obedient, the working of that plan is God's responsibility and not you're own. In other words, Keith and I have been called to be instruments of God's precious love to Michael. It is our responsibility to be obedient to God through availability. The final results of that love are between God and Michael. Keith and I are hoping that the results will be a young man totally surrendered to God and in love with His Savior, but even if he never accepts the love of God he has been shown, we must not "fail" to show it.

Love also never fails the Giver. We've learned through first hand experience that when you agree to let God love the unlovely *through* you, He never "fails" to make the unlovely lovely *to* you. Michael resembles nothing of the child who came to us that unforgettable Valentine's Day. Did the child ever learn to cry? Louder than anyone you've ever heard. The sort of weeping, wailing and gnashing of teeth that would make an ancient

Israelite proud. And, boy, did he learn to laugh. One day when he was in the first grade, I received a call from the Principal's office at his school. (I'm quite sure we're on speed dial at this point.) It seems that he walked into the boys' restroom during lunch while three little kindergartners were lined up at the stalls. This particular restroom had no windows in it so when he got the bright idea to turn off the lights, they reacted by screaming and turning round and round in a frenzy, thus effectively spraying the walls and one another. Michael was discovered minutes later still folded up on the restroom floor holding his knees to his stomach laughing until he was in pain. As I understand it, he was carried in that very posture to the Principal's office.

As you can obviously see, Michael is no longer painfully detached. He holds his own in the midst of a very active family. He vies for his rights but not nearly so often at the exclusion of another's. He adores his sisters and they adore him and they all seem to enjoy annoying one another to pieces. He tells stories with enough animation to make Walt Disney rise from the dead. And remember that tragic picture he first drew? Just one year later his kindergarten drawing of a Texas Longhorn won a district blue ribbon to pin on his boastful chest. He's miraculous, mischievous, and marvelously Moore. He still forces his teachers to earn their paychecks and his parents to stay on their knees. He is far more likely to get in trouble for entertaining other children than hurting them.

God has taught me things through Michael that I never learned in that Child Development course all those years ago. Three stick out in my mind above all others—

1) Perfect parents don't exist, but a perfect God does.
2) Agape is hard work. But it always works. It may not always have the results I want it to, but it will always have results.
3) Sometimes Agape really hurts. It broke the heart of God to demonstrate His love to us through Christ but its ultimate end was salvation.

There will be times that it will break our hearts to be vessels of God's love toward another, but its ultimate end is meant for salvation. The salvation of someone's soul, health, reputation, marriage, honor, sanity. Through love He saves.

To the Grace and Glory of our Rescuer Up Over, I believe that our son's life is good. Not easy but good. Michael has been forced to work harder at life in his few years than many others will in a lifetime. How hard he has had to try just to be normal may not mean much to others, but to a set of parents who knelt in desperation over a young child's bed not many years before, it means everything. When the ultimate "Award's Day" arrives, these will be feats that will not go unnoticed.

Award's Day

I went to my son's school that day
It was a very special day
When worthy tribute would be paid
To honor students in first grade.

Music ushered children in
Faces wet with toothless grins
Flags were raised and banners hung
Pledges said and anthems sung.

I stood with other moms in back
He didn't know I'd come, in fact
I didn't want his hopes set high
In case his teacher passed him by.

Every mom felt just the same
All had come to hear one name
The child she hoped they'd recognize
And find deserving of a prize.

The list went on page after page
As beaming children walked the stage
Cameras flashed and parents cheered
Grandma smiled ear to ear.

My eyes were fastened to just one
The anxious posture of my son
Perched at the very edge of seat
Too young to have assumed defeat.

Certificates for everything
From grades they made to how they sing
For days not missed, for how they drew,
Good citizens to name a few.

But it wasn't likely on that day
They'd honor one who'd learned to play
And stay in class from eight to three
Who'd learned to write and learned to read.

We hadn't hoped he'd be the best
We prayed he'd fit in with the rest
I knew no matter who they'd call
My boy had worked hardest of all.

An elbow nudged me in the side
A friend attempting to confide
A boy waving frantically,
"There's my mom! Right there! You see?"

They never called his name that day
I drove straight home, sobbed all the way
The boy? He had ceased to care.
He had a Mom and she was there.

LOSS

One of the greatest difficulties of Christ's earthly experience had to have been "knowing all that was going to happen to him" (John 18:4). He came to His own nation *knowing* they would reject Him. He loved Judas *knowing* he would betray Him. He spent intense hours with the disciples prior to His trial *knowing* they would forsake Him. Yet the depth of Christ's love and His willingness to face the Cross remained unchanged. In God's infinite wisdom, He chose for *us* to remain completely unaware of the experiences awaiting us. Sometimes we say, "If only I had known..." Far more often, we see the wisdom in *not* knowing.

When I wrote those last words about our beloved Michael, I had no idea he would one day return to his birth mother. As he approached preadolescence, serious internal struggles began to surface in the form of alarming behaviors. Although we never doubted Michael's love for us, he seemed unable to control many of his actions. In his childlike way, he was spinning in the cycle so aptly described by the apostle Paul. "I do not understand what I do. For what I want to do I do not do, but what I hate I do" (Rom. 7:15). Keith and I sought the expertise of countless doctors, specialists, and Christian counselors. We transferred Michael to one of the finest specialized schools in Houston and wore our knees to the bone, praying through oceans of tears. We were told over and over that Michael had needs beyond those we could meet. We asked God to confirm to us whether or not this counsel was true. We desired with all our hearts to keep Michael forever but knew if we were no longer helping him, we must find someone who could. To our shock and utter dismay, God confirmed He had a plan necessitating a drastic change.

Through circumstances so "coincidental" they had to be ordained by God, Michael's birth mother resurfaced, strongly desiring to reclaim her son. She was trying to put the pieces of her life together for the first time and believed she was ready to try to be a parent. Eight years earlier, I sat across a table from her in a restaurant and asked, "Are you sure you want us to have Michael? If you want to try to raise him yourself, I could simply help *you*." She admitted she was in no position to raise a child and granted him to us. As we drove away from that restaurant I cried to my husband, "She needs a mom as badly as Michael does." She remembered our conversation. When she resurfaced she said, "I want to raise him myself. Would you help me *now*?" Her name is Anne. She is not only Michael's natural mother but a close relative. We could not accept this sudden twist as simple coincidence. We did not make the decision to allow Michael to return to her for her sake. After extreme prayer and deliberation, we consented for Michael to live with her at least for a while *for his sake*. We pray and believe she holds an important key God wants to use in his healing.

I have come to a startling conclusion. In Christ we are capable of things we never dreamed. We have entrusted our boy to his birth mother's primary care. Through a grace and strength which could only come from heaven, I am attempting to do what Anne asked, to help her learn to be a mother to Michael. We are two women with absolutely nothing in common...except for one little boy we both call *Son*. We have a strange bond, and actually, a peculiar love for one another. We recognize his need for both of us and are both learning to share. I have never before experienced this kind of stabbing pain and loss. Words defy an explanation of the emotions my family has experienced.

We are surviving our loss on one solitary basis: we believe this is presently God's will. We wanted God to heal Michael in our home. However, God sees a grander picture. Another life is at stake here. Anne is learning to trust Christ for the first time in her life. She quickly confronted many difficulties but remains steadfast in her desire to do everything she can for Michael. I am proud of her. We have no idea what the future holds nor how much or how long she will be able to help. We have learned hard lessons about presuming permanence in terms of God's will. We know now that God always intended for Michael to be with us for a season rather than permanently. In my agony I cried out to God, "Why is this happening?" His answer came clearly to my heart. "For six years you have worked and on the seventh year you will rest." I was totally stunned. I realized God had planned this all along, waiting for a certain troubled birth mother to come knocking on His door. She came just shy of seven years. Our hearts are still in so much agony but our spirits are at rest. We believe we are in God's will.

I am so thankful I did not "know all things that were going to happen." I had no idea I would ever lose Michael so I loved him without restraint. I never dreamed he would return to his birth mother so I didn't love him like an aunt. I loved him like a mother. I fell short in so many ways. I wish I could have dozens of "do-overs" but I gave him everything I had. I will love Michael like a son until the day I die. We still see one another periodically and we hold on for dear life. We laugh and cry and try to understand. God has been faithful. He holds out healing to anyone who will open his arms and receive. May all who are involved in this difficult situation accept His healing. But above all, may one beautiful little boy named Michael call upon the name of the Lord and be whole.

The Life I Planned

Has someone seen the life I planned?
It seems it's been misplaced
I've looked in every corner
It's lost without a trace.

I've found one I don't recognize
Things missing that were dear
Promises I'd hoped to keep
And dreams I'd dreamed aren't here

Faces I had planned to see
Hands I planned to hold
Now absent in the pictures
Not the way I told.

Has someone seen the life I planned?
Did it get thown away?
God took my hand from searching
Then I heard Him say,

"Child, your ears have never heard
Your eyes have never seen
Eternal plans I have for you
Are more than you could dream.

"You long to walk by sight
But I'm teaching eyes to see.
I know what I am doing
'Til then, you must believe."

He's done so much, I felt ashamed
To know He heard my moans
To think I'd trade in all He's done
For plans made on my own.

I wept over His faithfulness
And how He'd proved Himself
How He'd gone beyond my dreams
And said to Him myself,

"No, my ears have never heard
My eyes have never seen
Eternal plans you have for me
Are more than I could dream.

"Yes, I long to walk by sight
But You're teaching eyes to see
You know what You are doing
'Til then, I must believe."

I felt His great compassion
Mercy unrestrained
He let me mourn my losses
And showed to me my gains.

I offered Him my future
And released to Him my past
I traded in my dreams
For a plan He said would last.

I get no glimpse ahead
No certainties at all
Except the presence of the One
Who will not let me fall.

Are you also searching
For a life you planned yourself?
Have you looked in every corner?
Have you checked on every shelf?

Child, your ears have never heard
Your eyes have never seen
Eternal plans He has for you
Are more than you could dream.

Perhaps you long to walk by faith
But He's teaching eyes to see
He knows what He is doing
Child, step out and believe.

*"No eye has seen, no ear has heard, no mind
has conceived what God has prepared
for those who love Him."*

1 Corinthians 2:9

Cost

These words are for anyone who has ever occasionally counted the cost of her calling by the drops of her tears. One of the high costs of my calling is God's requirement upon me to kiss my children good-bye and "go ye therefore." Every couple of weeks when I board another airplane, no matter how brief the excursion, I must trust my God to explain the "what for" of their mother's "therefore." I've found Him faithful. So far it has seemed that He is never more clearly there than when I am not.

Homesick

I called to check on home last night
To see if all was going right
My man assured me all was well
And it was true...I could tell.

I felt so far away from home
So by myself, so all alone
No noise here, no bouncing balls
No fussing kids, no endless calls.
I asked if everything was set
I didn't want him to forget
To take care of the "mother things"
To hang their shirts and crease their jeans.

He said, "Your oldest set her clock.
She'll get us up right on the dot
Don't worry, now, they'll get to school
We love you much, we'll see you soon!"

The phone went dead. I wasn't through...
I barely said, "I love you, too."
I sat and stared down at the floor
"She's never set her clock before."

She's just a kid, not old enough
To wake without a mother's touch
What chance is there at school they'll say,
"You're one great kid! You're loved today!"

Kids need to hear those words first thing
Before a careless clock can ring
And furthermore, they like, I frowned,
Hot cocoa when they first come down!

"Dads," I thought, and fell in bed
Then after while, to myself said,
"He's probably right, give them a break
She is fifteen, for heaven's sake."

"Fifteen," I sighed, "Where has it gone?"
Since that first day before the dawn
When she and I told secrets dear
And her first bath was in my tears?"

I'd held her close with just one arm
Reached for the phone to call my mom
"Oh, Mom," I sobbed, "I love her so!"
She cried as well and said, "I know."

The years are mean...they rush on by
The kite string slips into the sky
She's nearly grown, yes, plenty old
To wake up when the clock says so.

I felt so sudden like a fool
It won't take Mom to get to school
How silly...they will all be fine
Just go to sleep and rest your mind!

I tried to let the dawn go by
Without a call to check and pry
To see how every one had fared
Got your lunch? Homework prepared?

I finally grabbed the phone and dialed
It seemed to ring a country mile
My heart sunk swift...they must be gone
Dad's out the door...dog's on the lawn.

I started to hang up the phone
Until I heard a voice on
The other end, as up he leapt
"For heaven's sake, we've overslept!"

Suddenly the house lit up
He threw the phone, said, "Kids, get up!"
I heard each voice at a time
They were mad, but they were mine!

I cheered them on from miles away
I heard them readied for their day
And just before they slammed the door
She yelled, "Thanks, Mom!"

That's what I'm for.

Fragile
Places

Memories

There are times God meets us on our journey with others just as He did in my marriage, the birth of our daughters, and the adoption of our son. There are other times when God reserves the right to meet with us all alone. These are the times we search our personal worlds with desperation and find ourselves lacking. Times when closest of families cannot help and close enough friends cannot be found. Times when God Himself busies telephone lines, deafens ears, and blocks understanding. Times when He chooses not to reveal Himself through any living flesh but commands that you learn to look straight into His invisible face. These are times when we journey to the extremity. Times when answers never come nor would the end lest our "Why?'s" take us there and our "Who" brings us home. It's a place where we can only go alone. And find Christ alone.

My unscheduled journey to the extremity accompanied the restoration of traumatic childhood memories. Someone who should have loved me used me...someone who was a traitor to my parents' trust. Unable to process the memories until adulthood, the void had been filled with an unexplainable sense of shame and an insurmountable search for safety. Never delude yourself into thinking Satan does not prey on the lives of children. His wickedness has no bounds nor is any earthly ground sacred. He seeks to disqualify us when we're old by corrupting us while we're young. Often we try desperately to determine whether pain has come to us from the Throne of God or the Kingdom of Darkness. There is one sure way to know when Satan has been at work. SHAME IS THE SIGNATURE OF SATAN. As it was in the Garden, so will it ever be. Shame is Satan's "Been there. Done that." With shame comes the inevitable prison of secrecy. With secrecy comes loneliness. With loneliness comes poor choices of company. With poor choices come more shame. More defeat. More of the enemy. The strength of the chain intensifies and chokes abundant life. God has taught me that the secret to living is not living in secret. For there is where the shame is often bound. He used the recovery of painful memories and the reclaiming of my past, not to bind me, but to set me free. I arrive at this point in my journey void of the words you may be accustomed to hearing. Contrary to the claims of others, I am not glad it happened no matter how much I have learned. Only the foolish could make such judgments concerning crimes against a child. Certainly Christ would have no such expectation. Hebrews 12:2 tells me that He "despised the shame." I cannot fellowship in His sufferings without also despising the shame. But is also says "for the joy set before him" He endured. I have indeed discovered a taste of that joy and He was worth the inevitable journey. There is quite a difference between being glad something tragic happened and being glad Something happened out of the tragic. Through its lengthy course, when I could walk no more, I rested on the side of the road, rubbed my swollen feet and poured out my aching heart. These are just a few stops along my healing way.

Gently, Lord

Love me gently, Lord
I'm hurting now.
I've lived to see Your sovereignty
You've taught my knees to bow
I've caught glimpses of Your glory
I've seen Your righteous ways
But right now I need You, Father,
Just to face another day.

You have promised not to always be
Exactly what I please
But You give me sweet assurance
You're exactly what I need.
I need a gentle Father
And the lullaby He sings,
"Let Me tuck you safely
Underneath My healing wings."

Love me gently, Lord,
I'm hurting now.
You said, "Take Your cross and follow Me."
I beg, please show me how
To celebrate my weakness
That in You I might be strong.
When desperation grips my soul
A moment seems too long.

Oh, God, what noble plans I had
To do this whole thing right
Now I fall before You wounded
And I've lost the will to fight.
There are soldiers all around me
They're depending on me, too.
I fear I've nothing left to give
So, again I ask, Can You?

I'll love you gently, He says,
I know you're hurting now.
You've oft revered my sovereignty
Your knees have dropped to bow
If you could only see things
From My throne's clear point of view
You'd see glimpses of My glory
Are fast at work in you.

I'll love you gently. ·
Let Me soothe your hurting now
I've said, Pick up and follow—
I'll do more than show you how.
I'll turn this Throne of brilliance
Into a rocking chair
Crawl aboard, My precious child,
And I will rock you there.

Hide

Hide, little girl, beneath your Mama's skirt
Hide, little girl, and maybe it won't hurt
Hide from the laughter, what if it's at you?
Hide from the sorrow so no one has a clue

Hide, little girl, behind the smile you learned
Hide beneath the masquerade of credits that you earned
Hide in crowded corridors until the school day ends
Hide in courts of favor but never trust a friend.

Hide, little girl, behind your wedding veil
Eyes that cannot cry are eyes that tattle tale.
Hide, little girl, until your time runs out
Can't always hide, little girl, one day you'll be found out

You can run, little girl, to the only One who knows
To a place of fertile soil where trust can finally grow
Then you can hide, little girl, 'til every eye may see
You found, little girl, safely hid in Me.

"Hide me in the shadow of your wings…
that I may gain Christ and be found in him."

Psalm 17:8, Phillipians 3:8,9

Tricycle Dreams

Some dream of greatness,
      others of fortune.
            I dream of innocence.

And innocence has a face...
      cheeks pink with sunshine,
          eyes bright with hope,
             lips wide with laughter,

Propped carefree on the seat of a sailing trike,
      Curls bounce with the rhythm of percussions on parade.

Bare feet turn the pedals as she spies her destination,
      a trail of dust nipping at her heels.

No need to look back...there's nothing behind her.
      No past. She's only four.

She thinks tiny girl thoughts and makes tiny girl choices
      like how to dress up her doll.

Mama's best heels lay strewn in the grass,
      her pearls drape a tiny girl neck.

She likes Red Rover...
      likes for kids to come over...
         She'd rather go seek than hide.

She'll change her mind again tomorrow
      about who she wants to be
when three small wheels can no longer take her
      where she'd please.

And one day pain will surely come
      but it will greet her just as it should...
         by surprise.

Till then, fairy tales will consume her thoughts
      and trust will blind her childish eyes.

Yes, some will dissuade me and think it a waste
      and far too late for tiny girl dreams

But if through my prayers
      Christ gently spares
         One of these little ones,

Then dreams come true
      And there is innocence.

         Enough for me to share.

Extremities

Satisfy me not with the lesser of you
Find me no solace in shadows of the True
No ordinary measure of extraordinary means
The depth, the length, and breadth of You
And nothing in between.

Etch these words upon my heart knowing all the while
No ordinary roadblocks plague extraordinary miles
Your power as my portion, Your glory as my fare
Take me to extremities,
But meet me fully there.

64

Finer
Graces

Changes

I was an accident waiting to happen. The only one of my parents' children born without the benefit of anesthesia in the days when most mothers preferred the "wake me when it's over" method of childbirth. My very funny, ever so slightly eccentric mother reminds me quite often just how much I hurt. She calls me every morning on my birthday to say she has the cramps. By noon I've received some sort of hate mail from the postman. One year it was a card printed in Spanish. The only reason I pursued a B.S. degree in college rather than a B.A. was to avoid foreign language. Needless to say, I couldn't read a word of it and neither could she. In fact, it probably wasn't even a birthday card. The bottom was simply signed, "Love, Mom." Another year she sent me an ancient Christmas card she had found in an old box addressed to her from my Aunt Irene. It was yellow, brittle and ugly. She had marked through the words "Merry Christmas" and written "Happy Birthday." She even left my Aunt Irene's note at the bottom of the card, then marked out her signature and inserted "Mom." When all of us are at my parent's and someone suggests the kitchen needs cleaning, she's been known to remark, "Let Beth do it. She hurt the worst." And that was only the beginning.

Within a few minutes of my birth, I had an allergic reaction to the eye drops the doctor administered and I formed blood clots on the surfaces of both eyes. Not one of my siblings nor I had any hair until we started school and my skin was so pale and translucent you could see every blood vessel. Blood shot eyes, a bald head and see through skin. I looked like a shiny road map. I was lamenting my rough start to my Grandmother once and she replied, "Yep, people used to come by the house and peak into your bassinet and all they could think up to say was, 'Isn't she young, though!' "

About the time my eyes began to clear, the Army pediatrician pronounced me hopelessly pigeon-toed unless I succumbed to years of corrective shoes. They were the first things I put on in the morning and the last things to drop with a thud from the feather bed I shared with my grandmother at night. They were hideous. The soles were an inch thick. The colors were black and brown. When I grew out of one pair, I grew into another just like them. I longed for black patent leathers and bare foot sandals. Better yet, I wanted to be barefooted…a proud Arkansan's inalienable right. I wore those wicked things until I went into the first grade, long enough to have developed a life long shoe fetish. To this day, when I walk into my closet I want to see shoes. I don't care what color, what year, or what model. I want to see shoes. I don't care if they're not my size. I don't care if they're not mine! I want shoes!

The very week I got to shelve my corrective shoes, my older brother, whom I still adore, walked through the door and held his hands out to me. That was my invitation to go flying across that floor into his arms. And that is exactly what I did. Someone had moved a piece of furniture just enough to place a very expensive fold in our oval cord rug. With my freshly straightened feet, I tripped and went airborne. I landed mouth first on the edge of the coffee table, shoving my top baby teeth into the roof of my mouth. In no time at all, my teeth had turned black from the roots I had inadvertently murdered. I couldn't wait to get those horrible teeth out of my mouth so I could look "pretty" again. I knew it couldn't be long because I was at that age when children lose more teeth than their mothers do car keys. I jerked and jerked on them and, finally, one by one, out they came. I couldn't wait to grow in my new pearly whites. I woke up every morning and inventoried my top gums to see if there was any sign of them. After endless disappointing mornings, I awakened to a very strange sensation in my mouth. I just knew this had to be it. I immediately felt my gums and discovered nothing. I knew I felt something so I jumped up, ran to the mirror and lifted up my top lip. It was them all right. My brand new teeth. Growing straight out of my top gums. No, I don't mean bucked teeth. I mean teeth you could play chess on. Teeth that prevented my lips from touching for years to come. Teeth covered with some form of metal for twelve solid years. I feel sure I could qualify for the *Guinness Book of World Records* but who wants to be known for having the worst case of bucked teeth in the history of modern man? I had enough problems. The kids at school made fun of me and I had a heck of a time drinking my milk through a straw.

Just about the time I entered the fifth grade, my teeth were beginning to look somewhat southward. Then a horrible thing happened. It was something I had dreaded all my life. It had happened to all of my older brothers and sisters one by one. It was the generational curse. I thought fate might be kinder to me since, after all, bucked teeth should be the only suffering a person should ever need to mold their character. I was wrong. It's a wonder I didn't feel it happen. The night before it wasn't even there. I'm quite sure my head was a little heavier to pick up off the pillow but I've suffered memory loss over the trauma. I staggered to the mirror to brush my bushy hair and get ready for school and screamed. There it was. The family nose. And it was a doozy. My face practically had stretch marks. My eyes looked suspiciously closer together. It was bad, all right. It came from my Daddy's side of the family. The only good thing to be said about it is that it gets a little smaller with every generation. You should see his. As soon as he opens his car door at Kroger, the automatic doors open. They say his Dad had to be buried with an open casket.

In no time at all, "fish net" hose became the latest rage. They came in every conceivable color and, boy, were they cool. Goodness knows, I could've used a little cool so I saved my money and stocked up on every shade. Luckily, my mom was not like her stuffy friends. She cheerfully allowed me to make my fashion statement. There was just one catch—She wouldn't allow me to shave my legs. And did I ever need to shave my legs. The hair on my legs was at least an inch long and when I pulled up my fish nets, which took no small effort, I looked like an eighty pound porcupine in a chartreuse hair net.

By the time I was sixteen, I had been fired from my first job—assistant peanut butter grinder at "The Nut Hut." I accidentally ground my thumbnail into a patron's peanut butter. I might have gotten away with it, but my nails were painted red. Apparently my boss did not consider a broken nail punishment enough. These days a woman could sue over a thing like that.

I needed the Lord. In the midst of multi-talented brothers and sisters who had all somehow discovered their niche, no matter what my parents said, I felt ordinary and insignificant. Only one thing seemed to challenge my assessment. That man in those water color pictures my Sunday School teachers continually talked about. The One who calmed a sea, and more impressively a boat full of scaredy cats. The One who thought women were as neat as men. The One who surrounded Himself with children. The One I had accepted as Savior when I was a small child and found myself falling in love with as a young woman. No earth trembling testimony. No tale worth retelling. I met Him at home and fell in love with Him in Sunday School. For a little Cinderella who couldn't find her Fairy Godmother, He was my hero. My Knight.

As the years passed, things changed. I was no longer a nerd. I had grown into my nose a bit. (Trust me. I still show signs of nasal trauma.) Rollers calmed my hair. I was named everything from sorority president and All-Campus Favorite to Who's Who in American Colleges and Universities. Everything had changed. Except one.

"Jesus Christ...the same yesterday, today and forever."

Hebrews 13:8

I hadn't believed much of my own press. I still don't. Way down, deep inside is that same pigeon toed, bucked toothed little girl. And way up at my Father's side is that same Hero that touched the leper's spots and made him whole. And one day...

"...after my skin has been destroyed yet in my flesh I will see God. I myself will see him with my own eyes...on a white horse whose rider is called Faithful and True...How my heart yearns within me!"

Job 19:26,27; Revelation 19:11; Job 19:27

Heroes

In a world of philosophers, amateur and not
Exists arrival at a venue where agreement may be sought—
There are no heroes.

The young are oblivious to something worth defending
They rally 'round the reason on which they're all depending—
There are no heroes.

Statistics boast the aging are aging further still
While disease will never match the number emptiness will kill.
There are no heroes.

Where is the one 'round lines are formed
          for autographs worth sharing?
Who has a name proud parents steal and want their newborn bearing?
There are no heroes.

In a cold wet corridor through which a subway thunders
A young graffiti artist takes spray paint and wonders—
There are no heroes.

As lack of hope takes prisoners, if the soul within you shrinks
Let history bear her testament when you begin to think
There are no heroes.

To a man without a country, He appeared a joint sojourner.
To Joshua armed but afraid, He came a valiant warrior.

To Moses raised up on the mount, He was the One yet higher.
To Shadrach, Meshach, and Abednego,
          He was the fourth man in the fire.

To Elijah who stood as one for God, he was never less alone.
For Noah's faithful family, He made an ark their home.

To Ezekiel He appeared to be the light cast o'er the dark.
To King David running from the throne, He was the true Monarch.

To Daniel at the bite of death, He was the lock upon their jaws.
To King Solomon who'd had it all, He was the only worthy cause.

To a sinking fisherman, He was life upon the water.
To a grieving Jairus, He was life unto his daughter.

To a woman at the well, He was complete acceptance.
To a doubting Thomas, He was the proof for his reluctance.

To a dozen throwbacks from the world,
      He unleashed His awesome power.
From a greedy grave of several days burst forth his finest hour.

You may reply, "I don't accept such stark mythology
Written much too long ago—what have they to do with me?"

My friend, I beg you listen for in each there is a clue
What He has done for all of them He waits to do for you.

If you thirst, I know some flowing water live and able.
If you hunger deeply, He invites you to His table.

If your eyes are blinded, He's the One to make you see.
If you're in life's strongholds, He's majestic liberty.

If you're lost, He is the only Truth, the Life and Way.
If there is a debt you owe, there is but One who'll pay.

He is the Christ, Redeemer, the Son of God, adore Him!
He is the matchless, Holy One, and all will bow before Him!

So you may scale the mountains high
      and search the valley low,
But until you meet my Jesus, you'll search in vain,
He is the true Hero.

A Matter of the Heart

I've arrived at a conclusion,
Maybe one of life's rare finds
That there's not a lot worth salvaging
Within this heart of mine.

It's ever ready to destruct
And lie above all things...
It tends to laugh when it should cry
And mourn when it should sing.

I've wasted countless hours begging,
"Fix this heart, Lord, please!"
While it stomps its feet, demands its way
And floods with sin's disease.

At last, You're able to get through
And lay it on the line—
"You must give up that heart of yours
And trade it in for Mine."

So I cry out with the Psalmist,
Create within me, Lord
A new heart crystal clear
That only Calvary could afford.

A heart which pounds the rhythm
Of Heaven's metronome
And issues forth a boundless love
And beats for You alone.

I want to love that which You love,
Despising what You hate
And see myself as least of these
Oh, Lord, retaliate.

The efforts of the evil one
Who seeks to make my plea
That of his own, "I'll make no move
'Til I've considered me."

Peel away my fingers,
Finally make me understand
The power to love and please You
Can't be found within a man.

So, my Lord, I bring this offering—
A stubborn heart of stone
And ask You, in its absence,
Please exchange it for Your own.

How

How would I have known that I was lost
Had You not searched and found me?
How would I have known that I was blind
Had You not made me see?
How would I have known my bleeding
'Til You bound Your love around me?
How would I have groaned my slavery
Until You set me free?

Author, Finisher of my faith,
It all begins with You.
I'd still be wandering in the dark
Alone without a clue
That somewhere beyond the fairy tales
A child's dreams come true
Every time she risks her heart
And rediscovers You.

The Day He Called My Name

Schedules to keep, people to meet,
      it's a wonder I heard You at all.

Over city screams and midday dreams
      prevailed Your whispering call.

For only a moment, too brief a moment,
      You beckoned me up that hill.

Engagements were broken, apologies spoken,
      "I've a divine appointment to fill!"

I grabbed a canteen, threw a pack on my back,
      fully stuffed with all I hold dear.

Then I heard You reply with a smile and a sigh,
      "I don't think you'll be needing those here."

Piece by piece with sweet release
      The load dropped at my feet.

With empty hands on foreign lands—
      You chose that we would meet.

My feet fell stock on a steady rock
      and I began my anxious ascent.

The closer I came, the more I felt shame.
      I feared Your swift relent.

Yet as I reached the top, knees only to drop,
      You bathed me in glorious light.

My senses unhindered, eyes opened, heart tendered,
      Oh, what a beautiful sight!

"Just touch the blues, and smell the greens,
      and warm yourself in yellows"

"Savor the still, or dance if you will,
      in the shade of My umbrella!"

You spoke the Word like I've never heard,
      My spirit expelled such surprise...

The You I had known, had been gently shown
      Was transfigured before my eyes!

"Oh, Sweet Lord," my heart adored,
      "I beg You, please let me stay!"

"Come here, My child, let Me hold you a while,
　　For you must return today."

He extended His hand so that I'd gently land
　　On the path where I belong.

But refusing to retreat, I chose to leap
　　Falling from a cliff head-long.

He heard me weep, set me on my feet
　　kissing elbows I'd skinned and burned.

Saying, "There's only one reason for your mountain top
　　season—
　　Take to the valley all you have learned."

"But the pain's too intense, the noise immense,
　　I'd rather be up where You are!"

"That's the captive's cry," my Lord replied,
　　"the lost are down where you are!"

"Don't despair, I'm as close as a prayer...
　　I'll always descend to you."

"Let's fellowship sweet 'til your mansion's complete,
　　In the meantime, the mountains are few."

Though that time's come and gone, and life just goes on,
　　I'll never be quite the same

Since that day I remember, when all else surrendered

　　...and Jehovah called out my name.

The Treasury

We beg and plead and moan and cry
To make sense of this place.
We sweat and strive to fix it all
Then seek You just in case.
When will we learn to listen
To the Master clearly say,
"Seek treasures tucked into My Word...
It's there you'll see My face!"

Oh, hasten that sweet moment
When we'll know as we've been known.
Such secrets of Your glory
Cannot be grasped, they're shown!
This fleeting puzzle makes no sense
Except in You alone
And missing pieces swell our faith
And stretch us 'til we've grown.

The Company I Keep

Let me be known by the company I keep
By the One who determines each day that I greet
From the moment I wake 'til He rocks me to sleep
Let me be known by the company I keep!

Let me be known by the company I keep
When the valleys are low and the mountains are steep
By the One who holds fast when swift waters are deep
Let me be known by the company I keep!

Let me be known by the company I keep
By the One who implores me to sit at His feet
And quickens my soul to discern what is deep
Let me be known by the company I keep!

Let me be known by the company I keep
Eclipsed by Your presence that I may decrease
'Til all You have chosen this traveler to meet
No longer see me but the Company I keep.

A Momentary Rapture

The anguish of my humanness
Extends a ready plea
But for a brief encounter
Would You set my spirit free
To glide where words are meaningless
And earth's mere shadows vain
Where flesh is uninvited
And self is fully drained?

Please rapture me in spirit
Let me ride on wings above
To taste Your glory's sweet unknown
And bask in perfect love...
Where praise is not requested
But my soul's compulsory.
Draw me near Your presence,
Lord, disclose Yourself to me.

Let me rise above the stocks and chains
This body guarantees
Shaking loose the cowardice
Of my conformity
Call me, Father, summon me
To places never meant
To leave a visitor quite the same
When his sweet time is spent.

"Send forth Your light and Your truth,
let them guide me; let them bring me to Your
holy mountain, to the place where You dwell. Then
will I go to the altar of God, my joy and my delight!"
Psalm 43:3,4

The Mountain

I hear You call, "Come meet with Me,
See that which eyes are veiled to see
And ears in vain will please to hear
Except your heart should draw you here!"

"Abandon deeds down at My feet
No crowns as yet, no Judgment Seat
Surrender here all noble plans
Just lift to Me your empty hands."

"I'll fill them with the richest fare
And circumcise your heart to dare
To reach beyond all earthliness
For on this mount you're Mine to bless."

"With gentle hands 'til heart is stretched
I'll have My Word upon it etched
'Til only knees can catch the fall
Of one who cries, 'You are my all!' "

85

Seasons

Simple things...

Like a brisk catch of breath

in the first Autumn breeze,

Like pale pink buttercups

and a Springtime sneeze,

Like pink children's cheeks

on the beach at Summer's play,

Like praying it might snow

this year on Christmas Day...

Remind me that some things never change

Like Your unfailing love.

"As long as the earth endures,
seed time and harvest,
cold and heat,
summer and winter,
day and night
will never cease...
For Jesus Christ is the same yesterday, today, and forever."

Genesis 8:22, Hebrews 13:8

Heaven

How infinite Your grace for us
As You've prepared a place
Beyond our mere imaginings
With no familiar trace.
We'll find our custom built abode
Beyond the pearly gate,
Step by step down streets of gold
Oh, I can hardly wait!

Yet, Lord, I feel I must express
What Heaven means to me.
It's not the mansion of my dreams
That I receive for free.
You see, Lord, if You'd given me
A hut beneath a tree
Or led me to a country shack
Where I'd forever be

I'd make my home there happily
For always and a day
If You'd make just one promise
You, too, would come and stay
Because, My Lord, one thing is sure
So search my heart and see
It's not reward my heart leaps for—
You are Heaven to me.

Excellence

I am not about to suggest that either of the next two poems were inspired by tender moments with God. I would like to suggest, however, that sometimes life would be a little easier to take if we learned to steal a few moments out of every day to simply lighten up.

For today's frustrated woman, trying to do all she can do (rather than be all she can be), here's Biblical permission to resign a few activities—

"whatever you do, do it all for the glory of God."

1 Corinthians 10:31

Let's face it. None of us can do a thousand things to the glory of God. And in our vain attempt. we stand the risk of forfeiting a precious thing— EXCELLENCE. Oh, that we might discern the will of God, surrender to His calling, resign the masses of activities and sell out to do a few things *well*. What a legacy that would be for our children.

"And this I pray...that ye may approve things that are excellent."

Philippians 1:9,10

No where on earth is a woman's role more distorted than daytime television. This selection has been written in response to her example.

Superwoman's Freedom Plea

Oh, Lord, who said there's just One Life to Live?
I'm sure I'm livin' a thousand!
The few times I *do* awake to pray
All My Children start arousin'!

Uh, oh! No time for quiet now
Think quick! The day's beginnin'!
I'll try to recall all Oprah's advice…
Then my head starts spinnin'—

Make those younguns religious,
cautious but not suspicious
And watch their self esteem!
Yet you be professional, look sensational
And keep that house squeaky clean!

And perish the thought you'd forget the needs
Of that marvelous man you married
Why, throw yourself before him
when he raises his eyebrows
And quit thinking, "I'd rather be buried!"

Oops, now I'm late for work, the kids hate their clothes
And the baby's got a cough
As the World Turns so quickly, I'm severely tempted
To take the next jump off.

Surely they're kiddin', Is there anyone left
Who's honestly Young and Restless?
As for me, I feel centuries old, completely worn out
And cellulite infested!

It's gonna take more than Ryan's Hope
for this woman to survive.
I cannot abide another deep breath of these
Days of our Lives!
Superwoman? She's a curse. To fake her is impossible!
And if I try for one more day, I'll wind up in
General Hospital!

I've gotta be here, I've gotta be there
I frankly cannot face it.
Rescue me from havoc, please, show me what is basic!
Slow me down, Lord, save this life and
keep my eyes on You.
Satan can have this rat race world—

Thank God, I'm just passin' through.

Servant

Few of us are really confused about the issue of servanthood. Christ made Himself crystal clear when He said,

> "...whoever wants to become great among you must be your servant, and whoever wants to be first must be slave of all. For even the Son of Man did not come to be served but to serve and to give his life as a ransom for many."

Mark 10:43-45

For most of us the problem is not serving. The problem is that inherent in the title "Servant" is the inevitable "Servee." These words are dedicated to every leader who has ever wished that just one time someone would shut up and follow.

The Servant's Plea

Lord, I could be much better
As You would surely see
If I didn't have the folks to serve
That You have given me.
Yes, I could keep my halo straight
Above my little head
If coaching them to action
Wasn't moving tons of lead.
I would be so righteous
I would live my life in prayer
If You would kindly tell this group
To get out of my hair.
I would be so spiritual—
A Christian so much finer
If You would simply give to me
A flock without a whiner.
I wouldn't know how to behave
Without a tear to wipe
Or the chance to hurry to my church
And hear those people gripe.
Who cares on Sunday mornings
If there's donuts for the mob?
Give them something new to think
Or get those folks a job!
Yes, Lord, it's true, I'd love to serve
Beneath that lovely steeple
If You would take a good, stiff broom
And sweep out all those people.
What, Lord, is that You up there?
What's that I heard You say?

I said,
Your righteous robe is in a twist—
I'll untangle if I may.
It's clear you missed the point
While looking pious on your pew.
It's not what you can do for them
But what they'll do for you.
You see, My Child, some years ago
I signed this guarantee
To make you look much less like you
And far more just like me.
Take a closer look at them—
You'll see they are a gift
I'll use to reap your harvest, Child,
As grain from chaff I'll sift
And make you free to love them
As you have been so loved
So, go ahead, serve with a smile—
They're airmail from above!

Vulnerability

Without a doubt, the strongest emotion I have ever experienced has been in response to my children. There is little debate that motherhood takes a woman to the "breadth, length, depth, and height" of the human psyche. On a summer vacation in 1991, I sat perched on a large rock watching my husband and children prepare to take on the Texas-famous rapids of New Braunfels. Our three children, then eleven, nine, and five, all hooked up in inner tubes like little ducklings behind their father. Their bare feet were secured as tightly around the tummy of the one in front of them as they could wind them. The "shoot" seemed to jump up and grab them as they began their frantic ride through the rapids. As they dipped, swirled and spit water from their mouths, their expressions were so priceless that I laughed until my side screamed. Without warning the laughter suddenly transformed into tears. Not just any kind of tears. Overwhelming, uncontrollable tears. The attention getting kind. As people stared at me, I thought of faking a heart attack but I was afraid someone would try to give me mouth to mouth. I was utterly humiliated, but I was not confused. I knew exactly what had done it. I was dramatically and painfully confronted by the incarnation of my own vulnerability. There was my Achilles' heel...fashioned by the four people I love more than any others in the whole wide world. My life could be changed in the twinkling of an eye over any one of those creatures. In a second, my overwhelming love for them was transformed into excruciating vulnerability.

I cannot relate to any part of my Savior's perfection or His agony on the cross. The closest I can crawl into the backdrop of that pivotal scene in history is to imagine the emotions of that tender, naive mother. What must her thoughts have been as she stood below her own suspended vulnerability? I doubt this could have been a woman who stood in stoic control of her silent pain. Why would her Son have been so moved in the midst of His own ripping war with death that He cried out to His friend, "John, take care of her! Hold her! Lift her collapsing frame and assure her you'll be there for her! Do something!" Somehow I feel rather certain that this mother was just like the rest of us. She cried out for her own death to escape the intolerable sight of His. Suffering to hide her own eyes yet maternally unable to do so. She couldn't bear to stay yet she couldn't bear to leave. How different these moments must have been to "ponder" than those surrounding His birth. How she must have tried to shake the pictures out of her head for years to come. How she must have awakened and felt for just a second that it was all a bad dream. And she'd find Him back in that manger. Safe and sound. But it was no dream. It was a nightmare.

Since having my own babies, I have often wondered how different things might have been if God, in His perfect sovereignty, had allowed Mary to know the fate of her first-born Son. The stirring thoughts that run through my mind are simply summed—thank God it wasn't me.

A Mother's Thought
at Christmas

Had Mary known, just she alone, when in her arms a baby lay
The pain and sorrow of His tomorrow, sin in its ultimate display,
Would she have hidden Him and safely bidden Him
      and quickly run for His life?
Or could she have faced with no attempt to replace
      His inevitable appointment with strife?

What if she had known, through a vision been shown,
      the fate of His downy soft head
Which her cheek brushed gently as He cooed so contently,
      absent all feeling of dread
Of a day far too soon, the sun peaked at noon
      when men filled with hatred and scorn
Would puncture His skin and abruptly press in
      a crown protruding with thorns?

Had Mary known all along the fate of the palm
      she uncurled carefully with her thumb
The hideous sound that a hammer would pound
      when to a nail His palm would succumb
Would her grasp have grown tight as she clutched with her might
      each tiny, searching finger
That would stretch out in pain, no relief to be gained
      as the minutes 'til death only lingered?

What if Mary had perceived the message received
      in the swaddling clothes wrapped 'round Him
That they only foretold a body grown cold
      and the grave clothes that eventually bound Him?
And the clothes He'd wear from His body they'd tear,
      each garment from the other
As they cast their lots no mercy is sought.
      An eyewitness you'll be, Dear Mother.

As my mind still wanders over that one who pondered
      each moment in that stable
If she had known what Scripture has shown,
      would she have changed it if she were able?
I realize now as my knees drop to bow
      something of the God of Glory.
Had He told her these things, what Christ's future would bring,
      He would have told her the rest of the story—

"Yes, Dear one, who holds my Son,
      lifting Him from a hard, wooden manger,
He'll be a man of sorrows, all grief to borrow,
      from birth He'll be in danger.

On a tree replete with sin's defeat
   He'll soon die in your very own stead.
No earthly throne, He'll die alone, and thorns will crown His head."

"Grieve only a while o'er the loss of My Child,
   God incarnate in this baby boy.
The grave will soon see the captives set free
   and your heartache will turn to joy!"
The angels restate, "How long will You wait
   to give Him all You've longed for?'
My patient reply, First He must die…His grave is the Open Door!"

"As life came from the womb, there's life from the tomb.
   My plan is being perfected.
There's a place I prepare after sin I repair,
   for My children, My heart's own Elected…
Where all bow at His feet, death in defeat,
   and call Him the Lord of all lords!
Blessed choruses ring, 'He's the King of all kings!
   His Word a double-edged sword!' "

"For now, My child, but for a while, cuddle Him all you can.
Gather hay from the loft, sing a lullaby soft, 'Sleep, Baby, Blessed
   God-man.'
So much work must we do when time becomes due.
   Rest for now, My Darling, don't cry.
Stars, shine bright! Dance on His face tonight!
   Look up, your redemption is nigh!"

He is God's Son, the Only One through Whom men can be restored.
Dry your tears, incline your ears. Your pain is not ignored.

Hail His Majesty, the Prince of Peace, the Bright and Morning Star,
Bow each knee, and tongues proceed, Praise Him wherever you are!

Fresh Prints

We're inundated with the news
That all is at unrest
We've not a clue
What this world's coming to,
Just thank the Lord *we're* blessed.

Beloved, this very day
You thought you'd never live to see
Is just the one God preordained
And chose for you and me.

We're not called to shake our heads
And utter "what a pity."
We're called as candles on a hill
And towers in the city.

We can draw far more to Christ that tracts
Or fancy steeples
We are proof in breathing flesh—
God moves among His people!

Please understand, this race you run
Is not just for your prize.
Grab young hands, courageous band,
Run for their very lives!

For us, we must live for *today*,
For them, live for *tomorrow*.
Redeem the time for many blind
For there is none to borrow!

The prints of history's heroes
Will soon fade into the dust,
If there will be fresh prints, my friend,
It is up to us.

Footprints that walk the talk that says,
"I'll go where You will lead!"
Kneeprints that bridge the gap
And make the hedge to intercede.

God, kick us off our cushioned seats
Don't let us turn our heads!
Let's cease to hide behind the cross
And carry it instead!

You beckon us, "My warriors,
The time has come, ARISE!
Draw your swords, fight the fight,
Sound the battle cry."

"Where are My few who dare to say,
'Come follow Him with me?'
Would you lay down your own dear life
So that My Son they'll see?"

"Consider, Child, carefully—
Am I quite worth the cost?
To surrender hearts to holiness
And count all gains but loss?"

"I call you from your comfort zone,
Dare you be one of few?
If you'll not leave fresh prints, My child,
Then I must ask you, who?"

If you'll not lead the way, My child,
Then look around you,

who?

Steal Away

Steal me away like a child at play
To the fields that flow at Your feet
Spread the grass like a blanket cast
A picnic where two shall eat

For just a time let joy sublime
Serve our savory course
No fare of woes, no need for no's
Full without remorse

Animal clouds to guess out loud
Laughing at Your sky
You and me and I shall be
The apple of Your eye.

Time comes back and I must sack
What's left of fish and loaves
Some will taste with hungry haste
Steal away, steal away those!

Things That Remain

Faith—Knowing He can whether or not He does.

Hope—Knowing He will whether or not He has.

Love—Knowing He died whether or not we live.

Delighting thyself in the Lord is the sudden realization that He has become the desire of your heart.

Enemy

You have no power over me

          but what I give you

    no authority

          but what I bid you

    no voice

          but what I hear

    no leading

          but what I follow

    no savvy

          but what I ascribe

    no hold

          but what I cling to

    no skill

          but what I admire

    no room

          but what I make you

    no gain

          but what I hand you

You have

    no right.

My Every One

Lead me, Gentle Shepherd
Save me, Lamb of God
Feed me, Bread of Heaven
Alone on paths You trod

Hear me, Intercessor
Answer, Living Word
Rescue, O Deliverer
Still the waters stirred

Plead for me, my Advocate
Set me free, O Truth
Soothe me, Tender Comforter
Shake hell's kindred loose

Doctor, Great Physician
Seek me, Blindless Sight
Grant me, Freely Giver
Usher forth, Dear Light

Empower me, O Mighty One
Quiet me, my Peace
Keep me, Blest Assurance
From graven hand's release

Chasten me, my Father
Gracefully Restore
Build my house right next to You
Escort me home, O Door.

Echoes From the Pit

Come quickly, O my Caravan
The pit is dark and deep
My head is dizzy from the fall
My way is much too steep

Clouds obscure the fainting sun
Let night not catch me here
The well echoes my pounding heart
O, Caravan, draw near!

I stretch to listen...is that You
The rumbling earth restates?
Hasten please, O Caravan
Dark angels will not wait

I see the shadow of Your face
I feel Your knotted rope
Blessed sight, O Caravan!
Lifting me with Hope

Despised

My plane had arrived in Oklahoma City early that afternoon and I was not speaking until later that evening. I decided to take advantage of the quiet hours and study for my next Sunday School lesson. The text was Isaiah 53. I had been acquainted with the chapter since childhood and had committed it to memory as a young adult, yet in the moments that followed God allowed me to approach these words with a total freshness of Spirit. I meditated over the familiar passages that so perfectly described the suffering of my Savior. He was

> "despised and rejected of men" (v. 3)
> "...afflicted" (v. 7)
> "brought as a lamb to the slaughter" (v. 7)
> "cut off out of the land of the living" (v. 8)

The descriptions stung my eyes as if I had seen them for the first time. A picture so different from the one I usually imagine—The Great High Priest sitting truimphantly at the right hand of the Father interrupting my feeble petitions with power. It seemed so unfitting. The shame He had endured was nearly overwhelming to me in that moment. The prophet Isaiah was inspired by God to pen the definitive chapter on the doctrine of Salvation. One which answers so vividly the question of any God fearing Believer—"Is God satisfied with me?"

> "When thou shalt make his soul an offering
> for sin...He shall see the travail of his soul
> and shall be satisfied." (v. 11)

The issue is not God's satisfaction with man. God is satisfied with Jesus. One by one the descriptions moved me but there was a single verse that continued to steal me away with peculiarity. Maybe it was the woman in me. An inborn weakness for romance. An ongoing battle with vanity. I'll never know for sure; nevertheless, my eyes returned to those words over and over which described the Incarnation...the very "fullness of the Godhead bodily"*—

> "...he hath no form nor comeliness; and
> when we shall see him, there is no beauty
> that we should desire him." (v. 2)

*Colossians 2:9

No beauty? How can that be? My mind recaptured the familiar pictures on the walls of my fourth grade Sunday School class. His face looked so kind. His eyes so tender. His mouth turned up at the edges. His hair looked so soft. The pictures themselves had drawn me to Him. And to have seen Him in Person? How could He not have been beautiful?? Yet that's what Scripture said—to the human eye there was nothing beautiful to behold.

I sat back in my chair and stared out the window, imagining what it might have been like to have lived when He lived. And to have looked for myself. What would it have been like to have known Jesus personally? To have been the woman at the well. Or Mary, the sister of Lazarus, leaving Martha with the dishes. Can you imagine being the one about whom He said, "He that is without sin among you cast the first stone at her"?* Or the one who took the precious feet that would soon be pierced, anointed them and wiped them with her hair? Just imagine what it might have been like to have lived in a city called Jerusalem and to have known a man they called Jesus the Nazarene...

*John 8:7

Beautiful

You know, I've never been a person who saw things like anyone else. I often saw cruelty in the "harmless" games of children and poverty in the paths of the rich. I saw a joyous parade in the Kidron Brook as the water rushed the pebbles clean. So, perhaps I saw a different man than most. For You were beautiful to me.

Maybe it was Your eyes. Those eyes that showered fullest attention upon whomever You encountered. Eyes that fastened with such focus, I would have run...if I could've moved. Eyes that I realized knew everything there was to know about me. But eyes that reassured, "It is I, be not afraid." There was definitely something about those eyes. While the rest of us bowed our heads to pray, You lifted Yours straight to the Heavens, as if You could penetrate the endless blue and gaze upon the very Throne of God! But, then, You could, couldn't You? And when mine locked with Yours, I glanced into the very soul of God! Those eyes. They were so beautiful...so perfect...to me.

And those hands—how in the world could a carpenter's callused hands be so soft? Hands which could carve the most exquisite craftsmanship yet hands which could swing an endless line of giggling children running into Your arms after school. Those precious hands which broke the bread also calmed the raging sea. And to be touched by those hands? Oh, to be touched was to be healed! How I wish I could erase the memory of those hands covered with blood. How I had hoped those scars would be gone when I saw You again. Some scars are too deep to fade, I suppose.

And Your heart. Oh, I saw that heart in everything You did! The expressions on Your face. The laughter from Your lips. A heart from which You shouted in the midst of Your own agony, "John, take care of my Mama for me!" A heart which grieved the separation of loved ones. A heart which both hated and cherished the day when the grave would be overcome. Yours was a heart that pounded a passion for hurting people. A heart which ceased that the wages of sin might also cease. Your tender heart. It was so beautiful to me.

And who could forget that voice? The one which spoke the very worlds into being...and commanded the light to shine in the darkness...then *became* that light. The voice that thundered, "Lazarus, come forth!" The same voice that spoke the very imaginations of my mind and hidden sins of my heart...loudly enough for me to confront my own poverty...yet softly enough to spare my dignity before my peers. Simply, "Go and sin no more." The voice that tenderly called out my name. How I long to hear it again...That perfect voice which will someday repeat the invitation of a lifetime, "Come and follow me."

Yes, someday...maybe someday soon...the skies *will* roll back like a scroll and the angels will announce, "Hail, His Majesty, the King of kings!" And there You will be! In all Your glory! With unspeakable splendor! And all will adore You! And with certainty, the heart of every man, of every woman, of every child will fellowship in a compulsory refrain, "ISN'T HE BEAUTIFUL!" And, I, with no words to express, will joyfully...endlessly agree.

Perhaps love is blind. On the other hand, perhaps only love can truly see. Because, my Christ, my Hope, I want you to know...

You were always beautiful to me.

The Journal

I came across an old journal just the other day
Written twenty years ago—words that I had prayed
I sat cross legged on the floor and read its every thought
It chronicled my dreams and dares and battles I had fought.

Ink filled the pages with beginnings' dangled ends
College courses, roommate choices, countless boyfriends
I couldn't help but laugh at my astute ability
To transform such a simple life into complexity.

You'd have thought life's most important theme was knowing if or not
I'd get to know that brand new guy or keep the one I've got
Little seemed consistent in the life of one who wrote
Except the repetition of, "Oh, God, I love you so."

How on Heaven's Earth could I have known what true love was?
Surely youth obscures the wondrous works the Most High does
I held the journal to me and I thought of where I'd been
I sighed and cried to wonder,

    "And I thought I loved you then."

As if by a greater force I walked into the other room
Pulled out another journal—prayers weaved from a later loom
Ink filled the pages with beginnings' dangled ends
Cutting teeth, sleepless nights, and sticks from diaper pins.

"I think she said 'Ma Ma' today—I know that's what I heard!"
The moments seemed to slip away as quick as they'd occurred
One day I was the Queen of Hearts, the next I was in crisis
Monday my man was worth pure gold, Tuesday I'd quote his vices.
Little seemed consistent in the life of one who wrote
Except the repetition of, "Oh, God, I love you so."

How on Heaven's Earth could I have known what true love was?
Surely weary moms miss wondrous works the Most High does!
I held the journal to me and I thought of where I'd been
I sighed and cried to wonder,

    "And I thought I loved you then."

My hand reached for another in a more familiar place
Written by a woman with a far less youthful face
Ink filled the pages with beginnings' dangled ends
My oldest nearing college and my youngest turning ten.

This one struck my heart, its pages twisting as they turned
With lessons in the making and a few so harshly learned
My prayers were often moans and my questions painful cries
So many sick and hurting—time injures as it flies.

Relief would show up just in time through children's victories
Or sudden understanding of the ancient mysteries
Still little seemed consistent in the life of one who wrote
Except the repetition of, "Oh, God, I love you so."

No longer could I overlook the sole familiar thread
Quilting twenty years of ones—a single sentence said
How could I use those same old words to pen my fickle heart
Through ceaseless ups and downs and a thousand second starts?

How on Heaven's Earth could I have known what true love was?
I've only just begun to see the wondrous works He does!
His certain words fell on my ear as gently as a song
"Don't you see, My child? It was true love all along."

"Things were not so simple when you were just a youth
Your words told me the easy things, your heart told me the truth
And what more needful time for prayer than when a little one
Learns to mock your every move and bedtime never comes?"

"You needed me as badly then as you could need me now
The greater and the simpler both to train your knees to bow
Your words may seem the very same as those right from the start
But they fall afresh upon me when I see a different heart!"

"How on Heaven's Earth could you have known what true love was?
I met you at each step—for that's the work the Most High does
The times I patch and stretch your heart until it's nearly sore
Deepen you to say those words and mean them all the more"

"As surely as the ones which passed—we've miles left to go
Despite your inconsistencies, Oh, child, I'll love you so
You'll one day hold this journal, too, and think of where you've been
Ink filled pages tying those beginnings to their ends
You'll find those same old words—they'll puzzle you again
Lined face will sigh and wonder,

        'And I thought I loved you then.' "

After things pondered...
the dreams of a child,
the realities of an adult,
one thing remains...

Hope.

I've grown old enough to know
That fairies don't have tails
That good men often suffer
While evil men prevail.
I've tried to find that white frame house
With matching picket fences
But found instead black picket signs
And hatred's thorny fences.
I've lived enough of life to see
The innocent maligned
And I've concluded fairness is
A rarity to find.
I've seen the noble dreams of man
Be in an instant shattered
I sigh to see another woman
Used and bruised and battered.
I've seen shots of tiny orphans
As rulers rise and fall
I've stood by stricken parents
And caskets way too small.
I've abandoned childish notions
That life is like pretend
I've tossed paper to the ground and sobbed,
"When will this madness end?"
But I've never grown up quite enough
To leave my hope behind
I'll think I've turned my back on hope
Then bump into the kind
Of Gentle Traveller sent to bind
My wounded faith with love
Who sets my feet upon a Rock
And mind on things above.
Then I find myself still hoping
Old folks won't be left alone
And can't seem to quit believing
Daddy's still might move back home.
And that an orphan might just find
A reason to survive
And parents of the missing
Might just find their son alive.
No, I've never grown up quite enough
To scorn sweet signs of Spring
Nor can I help but think a tree
Is happy with a swing.
And you must pardon if I hope
The Pearl of Heaven's Gate
Is the treasure I've adored
And longed to celebrate.
I hope to hug the ones I've loved
And jump on cotton clouds

Where angels sing His holiness
And saints can laugh out loud.
Some bedtime tales are worth the tell—
May one be quickly due
Let Gabriel groom that great white horse
And board Faithful and True.
So let this world's prince mock and scorn
My hope is not ashamed
For in the King of kingdom's grand
My Hope has found a Name.